blished by
ACKPOLE BOOKS
neron and Kelker Streets
Box 1831
risburg, PA 17105

esign by Tracy Patterson
hoto by Judy Glattstein

the United States of America

ion

5 4 3 2 1

Congress Cataloging-in-Publication Data

Debra
erbs in the landscape : how to design and grow
erbal annuals, perennials, shrubs, and trees /
atrick. —

cm.
ographical references and index.
117-1187-0
rdening.   2. Herb gardens—Design.
rdening.   I. Title.
      1992
                          91-90155
                          CIP

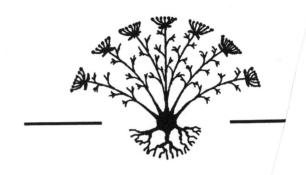

USING HERE
IN THE LANDS

How to Design and Grow G
Annuals, Perennials, Shr

Debra Kirkı

STAC
B

a
o
D
us

Pu
ST
Ca
P.O
Har

All r
or po
or me
inform
in wri
addres
P.O. B

Cover
Cover P

Printed i

First Edit

10 9 8 7 6

Library of

Kirkpatrick
Using
gardens of h
Debra Kirkp
1st ed.

p.
Includes bibli
ISBN 0-8
1. Herb g
3. Landscape g
SB351.H5K57
716—dc20

CONTENTS

Acknowledgments   vi
Introduction   vii

Herb Culture   *1*

Light
Temperature
Wind
Soils
Soil Fertility
Moisture
Planting

Plant Profiles   *27*

A Potpourri of Other Herbs
Herbal Trees, Shrubs, Vines, Ground Covers, and Wildflowers

Design   *129*

Foliage Color
Foliage Texture
Flower Color
Fragrance

Form and Structure in the Herbal Design
Form
Structure

Design Cues from Historical Precedents
  The Quadripartite Motif
  The *Hortus Conclusus*
  Islamic Gardens
  Knot Gardens
  Parterres
  The Kitchen Garden

Design Cues from Recognized Designers
  Gertrude Jekyll
  Roberto Burle Marx
  Beatrix Jones Farrand

Other Sources for Design Ideas and Inspiration
  Sense of Place
  Decorative Arts
  Nature
  Current Trends
  Intuition

Herbal Theme Gardens
  Colonial American Garden
  Fragrant Garden
  Culinary Garden

Contemporary Expressions
  An Herbal Tapestry
  An Entrance Court with Herbal Plantings
  An Outdoor Room
  A Garden for the Five Senses
  A Fragrant, Tactile Herb Garden
  A Culinary Herb Garden in a Raised Bed
  A Container Planting of Culinary Herbs
  A Modern *Hortus Conclusus*
  An Herb and Vegetable Garden Rooted in History
  A Rosemary Topiary Standard

An Early Spring Container Planting
A Container Planting of Contrasts
A Scented Hanging Basket
An Elegant Container Planting
A Planting of Contrasts Beneath an Airy Canopy
A Deep Green Planting Beneath an Airy Canopy
A Soft Planting Beneath a Dense Canopy
A Natural Garden
A Woodland Meditation Garden
A Planting of Native and Naturalized Herbs
A Rock Garden and Steps
A Knot Garden for a Small Space

Sources of Supply   222
Bibliography   224
Index   227

ACKNOWLEDGMENTS

Putting this book together has been an interesting adventure as well as a long and involved process. Along the way many people have helped. Tremendous thanks go to my brother, Richard Kirkpatrick, for his patient assistance, expertise, and all-around brilliance. I am also indebted to Dorothy Kirkpatrick, my ever-optimistic and energetic mother, for sharing her ideas and insights, sensitivity to the art and beauty of gardens, and sense of humor, which helped keep the book a fun and rewarding project.

Special thanks to my friend and colleague, Holly Harmar Shimizu, for her encouragement and assistance in horticultural editing.

I am also grateful to Wiley McKellar for his contributions in the writing craft, and to Jan Hahn for her artistic eye and the feedback she offered as I prepared the drawings for the book. I would also like to acknowledge others who helped and supported me along the way, including Bertha Reppert, Faith Swanson, Steve Harris, Leora Kirkpatrick, Peter Seidel, Bob Galaskas, Tom Hedenberg, Tricia Boothby-Melchert, David Melchert, and the talented editorial staff at Stackpole Books.

My appreciation is extended to the Herb Society of America and their Scholarship and Research Grants Program Committee for their part in supporting my work on *Using Herbs in the Landscape.*